FOREST BOOKS
CLOSED CIRCUIT

SHADAB VAJDI is an Iranian poet and linguist. Hitherto her poetic works have been published only in the original Persian. They consist of three publications under the titles 'A Bend in the Alley', 'A Song for Little Hands' and 'To the Memory of the Thirst of Southern Mountain Slopes'. This English translation contains poems from the last two publications, as well as some that have not been published before in either Persian or English.

Poetry has been only one of the activities of Shadab Vajdi. She studied Persian Literature and Social Science in Iran, and acquired her Ph.D. in linguistics at the University of London (School of Oriental and African Studies) in 1976. Her doctoral thesis ('A Transformational Approach to the Noun Phrase in Persian') was based on Noam Chomsky's theory of transformation. She has also translated Paul Harrison's 'Inside the Third World' and Liang Heng's 'Return to China' into Persian.

Shadab Vajdi

CLOSED CIRCUIT

*The poetry
of*
SHADAB VAJDI

*Translated from the Persian
by*
LOTFALI KHONJI

*and introduced
by*
PETER AVERY

FOREST BOOKS
LONDON ☆ 1989 ☆ BOSTON

PUBLISHED BY
FOREST BOOKS

20 Forest View, Chingford, London E4 7AY, U.K.
P.O. Box 438, Wayland, MA 01778, U.S.A.

First published 1990

Typeset in Great Britain by Cover to Cover, Cambridge
Printed in Great Britain by P.B.C.C. Wheatons Ltd, Exeter

All rights reserved. No part of this publication may be reproduced,
stored in a retrieval system, or transmitted, in any form, or by any
means, electronic, mechanical, photocopying, recording or
otherwise, without the prior permission of the publisher.

ISBN 0-948259-78-7

Translations © Lotfali Khonji
Original poems © Shadab Vajdi
Cover illustration © Katayoon Kianoush
Cover design © Ann Evans

British Library Cataloguing in Publication Data
Vajdi, Shadab
Closed circuit
1. Poetry in Persian, 1900— –English texts
I. Title
891'.5513

Library of Congress Catalogue Card No
89-85181

Contents

INTRODUCTION by Peter Avery	ix
My poem	3
Futile	5
The day	6
To the memory of the thirst of southern mountain slopes	8
On the city walls	9
The migrant storm	10
Garden flowers	13
The unfinished poem	14
Strewn with stones	16
The train	17
The moon	19
What's been left	20
Sobbing of the rain	21
The mist	22
Image	24
Sing me a song	25
Branded in memory	27
The pond	28
Hope	29
On the cross	30
I'm longing to see you	31
Your cradle	33
The little traveller	34
Why?	35
Poppies	36
Darkness	38
Clovers of love	40
The abyss	42
What is sorrow?	43
The bazaar	45
Let the heart go	46
Wound	47
The sound of distraction	48
A song for tiny hands	49
Set to depart	50

Greetings to the dawn	51
Tears	53
The most beautiful of all poems	54
Search	55
Even the wind sings your name	56
Our error	57
Flood of darkness	59
Explosion	60
In ruins	61
Crumbling structure	62
Distance	64
The bridge	65
I rain	66
Abadan	67
Since the day my name was called from among the winds	69
How to love	71
Need for a journey	73
Melody of two wings	74
Illiterate	75
Let there be light	76

Introduction

It is an honour to be asked to write an introduction to the English version of the Persian poems of Shadab Vajdi, whose very names in their Persian meanings suggest fluency of expression, both joyous and sad, and passion as profound as it is, in pure artistic discretion, restrained. It is also a responsibility to attempt, in a few lines of prose which must not be so presumptuous as to attempt to take the reader through each of the poems in detail, to explain how moving and evocative, of things Persian, of deserts that are part of Iran, of winds and fugitive flowers that speak of Central Asian vastnesses and those influences from as far away as China that are also part of Iran, these poems prove to be. For here we have that enamel-sharp brightness of imagery of which only an Iranian artist, poet or miniaturist, is so eminently and instinctively capable:

> *The wind*
> *swept every grain of darkness*
> *from the ground . . .*
>
> *We will take the stars home*
> *so they become flowers in the garden.*
>
> *The sun had gone*
> *but its clean blood*
> *remained . . .*
> *on the claws of leaves . . .*
>
> *God's green soul*
> *has been butchered on domes and steeples.*
>
> *Love means*
> *recognising the kindness of the veins of one hand*
> *from other hands.*
>
> *. . . the roads rolling back from cold deserts . . .*

This responsibility entails advising the uninitiated that they will in these poems encounter evidence of how perennial the artistic genius of Iran is. Yet, since this is so, it is in fact presumptuous anyway to give this work an introduction at all: the poems do not lack the power adequately to speak for themselves. In Persian poetry the universal is combined with and expressed through the particular — it is in all great poetry — and an allusiveness brings, as do Iran's clear night skies in a land where it is possible to read by the light of the stars when there is no moon, heaven down to earth, so that with the allusiveness is coupled startling clarity. It is inappropriate to refer to the 'uninitiated' since a Persian poem's universal appeal and gems of imagery must awaken something in the imagination of any reader who possesses the requisite vitality to rise and respond to any kind of poetry.

That the qualities characteristic of all great Persian poetry are brought to mind here means that Vajdi's demonstrates how that which is at once truly Persian and of appeal to readers everywhere may still, six hundred years after the death of Hafiz, drop from the lips of an Iranian. How perennial this art indeed is becomes the more remarkable when it is considered what a trauma Vajdi's Iran of today has suffered and from which it is still reeling. In this perhaps lies some, albeit seemingly paradoxical explanation, aside from the clear skies of Iran's elevated plateau, of the Persian poetic clarity: that, in a space between Asia and Europe, the Steppes of the north and Arabian desert in the south, Persian poetry has constantly, through a long history of vicissitudes, been an Iranian Phoenix — Huma is the Persian name for it — rising from the ashes, to proclaim the heart's continuing preservation of all that is of divine permanence, of the existence of which our only ultimate news is from the human heart and imagination.

Hafiz lived in an Iran that in the decades just before his birth had been devastated by Chinghiz Khan and his progeny. Vajdi carries in exile the ineffacable memories of public fountains made to run with blood-coloured liquid; of nights

> *. . . full of skeletons of corpses*
> *fearing the rattle of their own bones;*

of, in allusion to the Iran–Iraq War,

> *deserts feeling the weight of boots and corpses;*

of suns that set

> . . . *in pools of blood near our city;*

but this in a poem, 'On the city walls', in which the brave, lyrical plea is that poems be inscribed on city walls which by implication we are made to remember as from 1979 they were rendered hideous with vengeful, hate-filled graffiti. But the poet also remembers, and this above all, the persistent, haunting beauty of Iran:

> *travellers have heralded the sunrise*
> *and by the city wall dawn has pitched a tent;*

she will remember the smell of kebabs being broiled on a brazier at a doorstep where the family servant fans the charcoal flame, to dowse it and make it glow for the roasting of the meat. As is so much else, here too is the realization that earth is lovely but, not being paradise, demands a price for all its beauty and the wonders of life, so that the Iranians are forever aware that sacrifice is part of the glory of life on earth:

> *On the day I was hanged*
> *you were singing your own song*
> *not knowing that human shoulders*
> *were bearing the cross . . .*

lines which A.E. Housman would so perfectly have understood and might have written.

This poet's importance for us today lies not least in her presentation of the other, but still very Iranian, side of the 1979 Revolution: the eternal spring that, through rains of tears, weathers that worst of winters. The hope and the assertion of human powers of resilience are as Iranian, and as much the inevitable obverse of a despondency also peculiarly, and understandably, Iranian, as is that other Iranian phenomenon, for the salvation of Man, Sufism. The Persian Sufis are 'the people of the heart', *ahl-i dil*, and they know that 'a heart has the way to a heart', *dil bedil rah darad*. So, sweetly, does Vajdi:

> *but there is no separation*
> *between your heart and my soul.*

She also reiterates the Sufi position which acknowledges no boundaries, no creeds prejudicial to the heart's reflection of the Divine that is Man's supreme potentiality:

> *We are one and the same*
> *not knowing that august brains*
> *would soon brand us,*
> *in the dark and cloudy domains of their empty world*
> *into liberal or socialist,*
> *into believer or infidel.*

Whatever the immediate context might be, the message is one that rings down through centuries of Persian Sufi poetry; the message of the original equality of our origin in the Absolute One, and the equality of the spirit, God's part of Himself in the repository of the human heart, His secret treasury in His Image on earth. From this idea comes, surely, that of the life that 'turns into an unknown, mysterious impusle',

> *The same life*
> *that in my heart*
> *gazes at love . . .*

while material falseness crumbles, as does the bridge in the poem of that name, and, with the ancient Iranian conception of darkness as negative, the night, it may be remembered, was full of corpses fearing the rattle of their bones. Where an Iranian man or woman is truly a poet, the Sufi view of man and the world is always implicit; the spring from which utterance wells out.

But there is present the antitheses, light and dark, song and sorrow, the latter induces the former, flowers against dark soil, stars against black night, 'green plains' and the sun's 'mass of fire', which are a feature never lacking in Persian poetry. The thesis being advanced is that, whatever the difference in form between these poems, where the poet has broken loose from an ancient and extremely strict rhetoric, and those of earlier times, the spirit of Persian poetry still vibrates in these verses, so deftly and gracefully, perceptively translated by Lotfali Khonji. This thesis is urged, in particular for any of us who would despair of Iran, in order to show how out of place such despair would be.

There is an Iranian quality of genius that has conferred on the cultural achievement and imaginative horizons of mankind a special grace and that extension by which no less a person than Goethe knew himself to have been enhanced. The work of Shadab Vajdi, which Lotfali Khonji has presented in a form that does credit both to the Persian and the English languages, proves how the vitality of this genius continues to rise out of a degree of adversity which, in keeping with those Iranian contrasts already mentioned, somehow seems to make it stronger, as it turns tears into pearls.

Peter Avery
Cambridge 1989

Without the expertise and patience of my husband Lotfali, the task of translating this selection into English would not have been possible. My profound thanks should also go to Mrs Brenda Walker and Mr Mahmoud Kianoush who enriched the selection through their advice and their poetic prowess, and to Miss Katayoun Kianoush who further enhanced the selection by her design of the cover.

To those in my homeland
I have never forgotten

The Poems

My poem

My poem rose
and perched itself
on the branch of a willow.
In unison with swallows
whose breath was overflowing
with the changing of the breeze,
it began to sing
the song of life.

Life on the tip of that willow branch
and at that remote moment
was like flying
with two light wings of happiness.

Life was like a feather
at the mercy of mindless draughts.
It moved slowly round and round
in unknown space.

The blue, transparent bowl of the air
emptied light onto the field
with beauty and elegance.
The wind
swept every grain of darkness
from the ground
tidily, neatly.

My poem
at the heart of a fruitful cloud
above the roof-tops of a sleepy town
mingled with the breath of dawn
and was released
into the valley of its own loneliness.

It went slowly round and round
in unknown space,
and descended
to the side of every spring
full of clear water.

It descended
to the side of garden flowers
full of life and colour
. . . and, once again
it soared
and was absorbed into the planet of wanderings
was absorbed into the august tranquility of night
was absorbed into the ambiguity,
up and down,
sharp and flat,
that made music
with the movement of heavenly bodies.

It was absorbed
into the flight of a glowing shooting star
that, in the depth of motionless darkness,
was a streak of movement and vigility,
yet awake, aware.

On the cool roof-top of the night
the moonlight stirred
and my poem
was quietly whispering the song of life to itself.

Futile

Ignorant graveyard priests
have uttered their final, mortal pronouncement
on life
and sent all our dear ones
to the slaughterhouse of war,

... and
comrade Morteza
in a Paris street-corner café
breathing Parisian air
blended with smoke from 'Winston' cigarettes
ruminates worthless philosophy
in his latest ideological analysis
and philosophises
on the confrontation of the bourgeoisie
with the proletariat.

Alas ...

The day

I see the day
alighting on tip-toe
on roof-tops
and on tops of trees

I see the day
spreading itself along streets
caressing
the sleepy eye-lids of windows.

Now
patches of cloud
are set afire
but the first flames of the sun
and the promise of a sunny day
are read
on the high forehead of the sky.

Now
the first passer-by
walks through the streets of light
and the purity of the sky
is crystallised
into dewdrops
and into eyes of little windows.

I see the day
seeping through my mind's filter.
In its dazzling light
everyone's face
is as clear and as naked
as a mirror.

And . . . the hands
the movement of the hands
is the movement of hidden moments
telling the untold.
I look, I stare
and
tired and broken-hearted
rest my head
on the shoulders of loneliness.

روز

روز را می‌منم
که پاورچین
بربام خانه‌ها
و فرازترین شاخ و برگ درختان
فرود می‌آید

روز را می‌منم
که خود راهبن می‌کند
در طول خیابانها
و پلک خواب‌آلود پنجره‌ها را
نوازش می‌دهد
اینک
پاره‌های ابر
در اولین شعله‌های خورشید
می‌سوزند
و نوید روز آفتابی
بر پیشانی بلند آسمان است

اینک
اولین عابر
از خیابانهای روشنایی می‌گذرد

و پاکی روز
در دانه‌های شبنم
و چشمان دریچه‌ها
متبلور می‌شود

روز را می‌منم
که از صافی ذهن من می‌تراود
و در روشنایی خیره‌اش
سیمای هرکس
به عریانی آینه

رو بروم
و .... دستها
حرکت دستها
حرکت لحظه‌های نهانی است
که بازمی‌گوید
همه حرفهای ناگفته را

نگاه می‌کنم ، نگاه می‌کنم
و خسته و آزرده
سر بر دوش تنهایی می‌گذارم .

To the memory of the thirst of southern mountain slopes

I can hear the rain
I can hear the rain
It has been raining all night,
and my heart has been singing all night
in the memory of the great salt desert
thirsty as ever for every drop of rain
in memory of southern mountain slopes
in memory of droughts and their heart-breaking
                                            remoteness
in memory of the innocence of the familiar soil,
                            so close to my heart.

It has been raining all night
the whole town is filled with the melody of rain
my whole memory is submerged in your distant voice
the tiniest particle of your soil
is my dearest jewel.

I can hear the rain
Behold! Here, in memory of your soil
I rain in unison with bountiful clouds
rise in loving hope of greener spring-times
moments of budding are the dearest ones
and the spring-time yields
springs of uniform, clear water.
Rise in loving hope of greener spring-times
your spring-time will be mine too.

On the city walls

Inscribe your poems on the city walls
so that every passer-by can read it
so that the sun
washing her face in sea water in remote regions
and in pools of blood near our city,
can read it too.

Inscribe your poem on the city walls,
travellers have heralded the sunrise
and by the city wall dawn has pitched a tent.

I was twenty years old
the day they hanged me on the gallows
I was not alone
but the youngest among friends.

On the day I was hanged
you were singing your own song
not knowing that human shoulders
were bearing the cross.

A fire burning far away
is a sign of life
above all these plains
and above the silence of all this green
the sun shines
and shines
even on that high hill
where death stands —
it shines.

Oh, how I bade farewell to the city
to the little shops
to the narrow alleys
where the lamp-posts were the only symbol of light,
the lamp-posts I used to count each day.

Oh, how I bade farewell
to the frightened people
afraid of feeling
each other's existence,

how I bade farewell to my family home
to that familiar neighbourhood
whose trees,
every branch of them,
were my friends.

You are still singing your own songs
still loving yourself
but my eyes are in love
and my young heart
seeks the steepest paths.

On the day they hanged me
it was as if life began
as if the old tree
felt buds growing on its old branches
as if dawn broke
and the city woke.
Light was no longer symbolised by lamp-posts.
Our corpses
on that high hill
danced with the breeze,
death was not the end of the road
it heralded a beginning
and like stars on the sky
there were bloodstains on the earth.

The migrant storm

In the tight world of the cradle
my first feeling was the kindness
of tender motherly fingers,
from that moment
I was linked to the perpetual vein of humanity
in East, West, North, and South.

On that day, all the babies
cried with the same needs,
cried for hunger
and all our little eyelids
saw us off
to the threshold of sleep
to the gates of night,
not a line was seen on our little fingertips
not a single label on our innocent foreheads.

We were one and the same
not knowing that august brains
would soon brand us,
in the dark and cloudy domains of their empty world
into liberal or socialist,
into believer or infidel.

Oh brothers!
I am the migrant storm
blowing from East to West
from North to South
covering all continents, all horizons
I can't be bound in your tight empty world.

Oh brothers!
I am a vast ocean
washing and dissolving all colours
submerging all darkness,
I can't be bound
within your artificial moulds
separated from the rest of humanity,
I am human
from the day I was linked to that perpetual vein

my heart breaks at the sight of people
bound by chains of fanatacism and blind commitment,
my heart breaks
at the sight of a human face
facing execution
at the sight of the human skull
shattered by stones.

Leave me alone
forgive me for seeing humanity whole
unbound
indivisible.

Garden flowers

With your kisses, garden flowers open.
With your kisses, the nocturnal sky is filled with stars
and even day is filled with luminous atoms.

With your kisses, the spring garden comes to life
and the fiery sun of the South
in the blue sky of the shores of the Qeshm Island[1]
shines once more.

You are from the South
whose days are hot
and whose nights have skies overflowing with stars.
You are from the South
and that is why
rays of kindness shine upon our rooftop.
How kind, how warm.
For me
it's as if spring-time is blossoming.
For me
the entire soil is covered with wild tulips.

---

[1] An island in the Straits of Hormuz

The unfinished poem

Tonight, write a poem
that would be the greenness of all trees
and the redness of the beating of all hearts
whose beatings you can still hear from afar.
From beyond frontiers
from beneath the earth,
they have embraced lead bullets.

As you see,
the night spreads
within and without the frontiers
beyond the seas.
As you see,
the night spreads
along all streets
where men tired of life
are taken away by it to the chalice
and are submerged by it.
It spreads
to the top of all skyscrapers
that give refuge to those men's motionless feet
                                and wandering souls.

The night spreads
even above the heads of those
whom you imagined as the followers of dawn.
It spreads
in the looks of all those
whose looks you imagined
as the prayers for the dawn's kindness
whose looks you imagined
as the melody of rain for the seeds of a love song.

So tonight, write a poem
that would only be
the greenness of all trees
and the immortal resonance of waves
that wash the filth away from night.

So tonight, write a poem
but leave it unfinished
because one must wait and wait
in patience
until the seed sprouts
because one must listen and listen
in patience
to the beating of broken hearts
until filth is washed away
and the night is vanquished.

Leave your poem unfinished
because everything on earth is unfinished
I mean every good thing
everything worth starting.
All those unfinished good things
are taken further ahead
by the beating of hearts
and are spread
even beyond time itself.

Strewn with stones

I was on my way
when nightfall worried the sky
when darkness plundered the sun

The muezzin's voice
is no refuge
to strangers travelling at night
the muezzin's voice
has only taught them to weep
the road remains dark and obscure

The one who smiled
was a stranger
and the one who aimed at setting foot on the
                                mountain ridge
leaned on a walking stick,
the strangers travelling at night
started to weep imagining the end.
Whoever looked for his own home
had an unfamiliar address in his hand

By-ways joined the night
so did the lagoons
I was on my way
there were no more lights
there were no more voices.

Oh, you, wandering stranger!
Behold! See how the clouds weep
and how clean are their tears.
I was on my way
when on that stony ground
no hands stretched out to help
when everyone hid his darkness
when everyone hid his own thirst
when everyone was lost on his own way

Oh, you wandering stranger!
I love the desert
and tears
for they are clear and genuine.

The train

Filled with the racket of anxiety
with wheels gliding over rails of doubt
the train is taking me towards you.

It seldom arrives on time,
I am content
merely to cast a second glance at life
from its windows
a second glance at people
waiting at stations
for a train
to take them to their destinations,
at people who have forgotten
how to walk on their own feet.
The train that takes me towards you every day
is filled with anxiety.
In its little compartment
not a cigarette can be lit
to kill the anxiety
or to gaze at life's eyes
from behind the grey smoke.
I am content
merely to cast a glance
at plains and harvests
at sheep moving towards their pens
at horses grazing free from worries
at lines adorned with washed clothing
at houses behind whose doors
life goes on so quietly.
The same life
that in my heart
turns into anxiety
turns into an unknown, mysterious pulse
turns into a rapid current
that carries everything with it
turns into an explosion
whose sparks fill the night with stars.

The same life
that in my heart
gazes at love

and turns into despair,
the same life
towards which
my eyes are fixed in anxiety,
the same life
that does not let me sleep quietly
because in my head
it reverberates with the rhythm of the train,
the same train that takes me towards you
every day.

The train that takes me towards you every day
has passed over bridges of friendship
and it will continue to pass
over bridges of friendship.

But alas!
It puts me down before reaching the last station.
Having forgotten how to walk on my own feet,
I go astray,
I am afraid of losing my heart
with its unknown, mysterious pulse
along the wrong road
without my feet having learned to move
and to replace the gliding of wheels
                              on the rails of doubt
with the footsteps.

The train that takes me towards you
has wheels filled with the racket of anxiety
strangely,
the same train
takes me further away
further away from you.

The moon

The moon
The great moon
The big, red moon
The moon that reminds me of childhood skies
of roof-tops in summer[1]
of the flowing tales of water
lurking in the lonely soul of night.

The moon
The gypsy magician
shining over the summits of pride
resting on the white clouds of serenity.

The moon
The moon of childhood tales
The good moon
The sad light of back alleys
The moon of the heights of Touchall[2]
The moon of the endless valleys of the Alborz[3]
Gazing over the extinguished light of the town
over the passage of years.

The patient, silent moon
The moon of the eyes of mothers
waiting on the roads rolling back from cold deserts
deserts feeling the weight of boots and corpses
The moon gazing in astonishment
at so much atrocity
The wandering moon
The quiet moon
walking on tiptoe . . .
The moon . . .

---

[1] In most regions of Iran, it is customary to sleep on roof-tops in summer.
[2] A mountain to the north of Tehran.
[3] A mountain range in northern Iran (to which Touchal belongs).

What has been left?

The darkness is penetrating
The darkness of night is flowing inwards
And my helpless glance is wandering
along the dark paths of the sky.

I am thinking of the logic of the wind
that tore flowers into petals
for no reason.

I am thinking of the logic of the night
that spread itself equally
over plains and deserts.

The dark paths of the sky
are devoid of the birds' flight
and the silence of confused paths of the earth
is not broken by any footstep.

What am I looking for
beyond the window?
And what's remained of me
but a heart
that still loves loving?
What else has remained of me?

From afar
I can hear a voice,
it's my mother's voice.
It's just a sigh
there must be a wound
there must be a pain
hidden by the night.

My feet are too weak to go on.
My feeble hands
are striving with the huge mass of darkness
trying to make headway through the night.

In my struggle to reach that voice
the last particles of my life
fade.
And what's remained of me?

Sobbing of the rain

Out of so many hearts
that beat at the lower depths
of the inferno of terror
why are no shouts or cries rising?

Oh you! The dark silent night of the dispossessed
tell me, how many little nests
were destroyed by the hands of this hurricane?
Tell me, how many blossoming trees
turned to dust?

The sobbing of the rain is flowing in the alleys
Tell me, night!
Are there any sighs left in the moon's broken heart
behind the dark masses of the clouds?

There are one thousand leagues
between my body and yours
but there is no separation
between my heart and your soul,
I feel whatever you suffer.
There is no salvation for me
from so much pain and tyranny.

You are in chains
You are in the claws of inhuman beings.
Oh, God!
Why is there no voice
from within that dungeon?

Break the silence
for the night shall not last.
Beg the sun to rise
if you are awake.

Anger wants to force life out of my body
when I recall so much bestiality,
so much deprivation.

Out of so many hearts
that beat at the lower depths
of the inferno of terror
why are there no shouts or cries?

The mist

The forest closes its eyes
and the sadness of the mist
penetrates the veins of a winter sunset.

Oh, what dark and heavy moments!
The road has lost sight of its own track
in the sadness of the mist.

The light from afar
escapes from closed, blind minds.
Oh, what cold and bleak moments!

The delicate petals of the sun
have taken refuge in an empty valley
from fear of darkness.
Little petals of the sun
like trembling flames
in the claws of a storm.

I, like a worthless particle,
rise from the curve of the hill
with the dust of the road
in the sadness of the mist
and I land among the crowds of the town.

In the narrow alleys of memories
no hawkers can be heard, no playing children.
In the meagre, dusty alleys
short, silent doors
wait for a hand to open them
and roof-tops still wait
for the flight of pigeons.

With the dust of the road on my eyelids
I carry my loneliness on my shoulders.
I am looking for a door
that will open
without being knocked.

From the roof-tops
the chant of 'God is Great' can no longer be heard.
Perhaps God has stepped down
from His celestial glory.
Perhaps He has been swept away
by floods of human tears
on both sides of the jail bars.

Perhaps He has, in shame,
thrown Himself down
from roof-tops of mud houses
or, even, from the height of green minarets.

Or perhaps
He has remained buried
under mounds of corpses.

In the sadness of the mist
I descend from the hill-side
and land among the crowds of the town
I intermingle
with the dust of empty alleys
and, together with rain-drops,
flow
in the old veins of the town.
I flow
in the cold sighs of human beings
sighs that are spread
like the sadness of mist.

Image

Every day, a raven
sitting on the leafy branch of the old plane tree
heralds the death of the day with its harsh cawing.
In the frame of the open window
its image
its black image
on the green canvas of leafy branches
is like an old work of art.

I think this painting
is the work of a dead artist.
It is evident
that this black cloudy sky
is awaiting bitter grief . . . hard weeping.
It is evident that
this impatient black-winged raven
is sitting there awaiting its mate.

This day is over too
but still the raven
that lonely, mateless raven
and the dark cloudy sky
do not believe that the painter is dead
and that
the sky with its dark grief
and the raven
must remain mateless forever.

In the frame of the open window
is an old painting
that has gathered much dust
it is an image
 . . . .of time
 . . . .of destiny
 . . . .of waiting in vain.

Sing me a song

Sing a song.
For me,
along the rugged, stony paths of loneliness,
along the tree-lined lanes of a sad night,
sing a song.

At the fixed hours of life,
and the confined stations of time,
no longer does the whistling of trains
end my waiting.

Among the turbulent waves of what night,
around the orbit of what wandering,
can you search for so many answers?

Sing me a song
of the rustle of fallen leaves,
of the paces of passers-by,
of a stranger's mark on passing years,
like footprints on snow.

Sing me a song.
The night is full of unfortunate corpses
with faces strange to their owners.
The night is full of skeletons of corpses
fearing the rattle of their own bones.

Along this dark path,
the sun will never return to the East
from his journey to the bamboo-fields of the sunset.
And the sunrise is a song
lost amidst the blood-soaked gorge of the sky.

Sing me a song.
The moat was waiting mouth wide-open
for human bait.
Oh, sad little corpses.
The moat looked like a tomb
on the fever-stricken body of the desert.
Oh, the wounded with the burns.

Along this down-hill descent,
I know figures
that weave robes of power
from burnt wounds.

I come from a land
whose inhabitants, old and young,
have fallen asleep
on the soft pillows of their ideologies.

At the fixed hours of life,
at the confined stations of time,
why do you not see
that your laughter
is but the laughter of vultures
at the corpses massed in the moat?

Does one have to rub
the dark clouds in the sky
against each other?
Does one have to wait
for a very long time?

Sing me a song
that would herald the emergence of storms
and the downpour of sunlight
on the vast expanse of the East.

Branded in memory

The sun melted gold.
In the red and violet sky of the dusk
so many cloud patches
were burnt in the flames of the sun's torch.
On the dry branches of garden poplars
birds gazed at the colours of the horizon.
And sunset lent a tinge of red
to the autumn-stricken faces of the leaves.
One side of every leaf was golden
and the other side fiery.
The orange of the sunset spread across the sky
and the white calm of my heart suddenly broke.
The sun had gone
but its clean blood
remained
in the heart of the sky
on the claws of leaves
and in the chalice of gloomy ponds
— branded in memory on my impatient heart.

The pond

Oh, heart!
Oh, heart!
buried like a pond in the solitude of night!
Tonight the moon will be broken into two halves.
One half will descend on you,
the other
will tie the night
with unhealed agony.

Oh, heart!
I tear open my chest
and press you in my hand
so that all agonies
drip down drop by drop
and the tears that were imprisoned for years
mix with fertile soil.

The song of all birds
when the sky is full of flight
are within you.

The sound of breaking branches
at the time of storm
are within you.

The sound of the springtime
walking in the corner of the forest
and the song of the lonely wings
of multi-coloured butterflies
are within you.

I tear my chest open
and running, take you
to the heights of the sun
so that the roots of light
penetrate your body, your soul
so that the sun germinates
in the infinity of your life.

Oh, heart! You are buried in the solitude of the night.
I will raise you, take you to the sun.

Hope

Far, far away, tonight
the gates of the horizon open
and all the stars suddenly fall.

With cupped hands
I have been awaiting their descent
for so many years.

Let me catch them all
don't let even one go astray.

We will take the stars home
so they become flowers in the garden.
We will take the stars to the city square
among the crowds.
To the empty heart of each of them
we will give a spark
as a gift
and, thus,
the dark city
will attain salvation.

On the cross

For so long,
I have been detesting myself;
for I have no strength
to fight the anti-human tribe.

I cannot penetrate the stone of their brains
in the quagmire of their foulness.

Shame on us
who still breathe
far from that unhappy air scented with tears.

Shame on us
who still walk
far from that unhappy land, drowned in blood.

Shame on us
who have forgotten the last glance of friends
at the gates of farewell to light.

Shame on us
who have made peace with deceit
smiled on the face of falsehood
and accepted surrender.

Nail my hands
to the cross of shame.

Nail these hands
that cannot tear the chains of torture
from that beloved body.

Nail these hands
that cannot wipe away the stains.

Nail my hands
to the cross of shame.

I am longing to see you

I am longing to see you
I want to see how you open your eyes to the dawn
I want to see how you practise your first steps
along the difficult path.
Oh! My little sapling!
You blossomed when little seeds
pushed the soil back
in order to see the sun
and when buds
cracked the brittle husk of tree trunks
in order to feel the breeze.
But . . . alas
when you blossomed,
it was also the time
when your mother felt tired in mid-way
when there was little light
when darkness was dominant
so dominant
that particles of human bodies
fused with it.

You will be born in pain
I wish your tiny heart
will forgive the sin of a mother
whose sin is to bear you
in the middle of darkness.
You will be born in pain.

Oh! My little sapling!
Oh! My genuine, truthful poem!
I want to see you.
The forests are overflowing with the hubbub
from the flutter of little birds
the greenness of the meadow is green and untarnished
and I love all this
and I think
that tarnish and ugliness
only belong to human beings.
I wish you were born of nature
I wish you were a tiny rain drop,
dripping from clean clouds
I wish you were the small petal of a blossom
that would open with the wind.

Be a rock
be the serenity of the sea
and the cleanliness of the meadow.
Behold how my tears come down
from the guilt of bearing you
and how my back is bent under this load.
Up to what point will you carry the cross
Oh, my little Christ?

Your cradle

When the eyes of leaves were tearful
you came to learn how to smile
when tears were dropping from leaves
you came to obliterate dark shadows.
The leaf that was tearful
now feels nothingness
and you
fuse your smile
with the blossoming of your lips.

    *   *   *

The sun was like a crop of abundance.
The sun was like a mass of fire
I wish the sun were your cradle.
With you, I will traverse green plains
and, together,
we will feel the sides of the brook
lined with delicate plants,
together
we will feel the signs of simplicity and beauty.
The moon is God's moon
and nature is His nature
and we, like little plants,
will not fear the storm despite our weakness.
You are not afraid of hardened feet, are you?
You dislike delicate idle hands, don't you?
You know how
dry deserts are longing for rain
and how
high mountains
preserve the echoes of thunder
in their strong chests.
You know how
slime forms in stagnant water
and how
stench rises from closed spaces.
I will traverse open plains with you, step by step.
Together
we will follow the movements of the wind.

The little traveller

Before the cricket sings its lost song
into ears of the moon
and before the apple tree
offers its last fruit to the wind
I will hear the beating of your tiny heart.
Oh, my little traveller
there is no waiting, no longing
like the one to see you.

I have already opened the windows
I will call the sun in
so that from the first moment
you will meet with light and freshness of the air.

I have already woven your little socks
and the road
is awaiting the steps of yet another traveller.

* * *

Along the path of the wind
nothing grew but a little bush
and from then onwards
the wind sang all her love-songs
in thought of its presence
and filled the whole length of the night
with singing.

Why?

On tiptoe
the night approached the private gathering
of wild flowers.
And the moon's tears
dripped on the cold faces of ponds.

Think of the earth.
The winds of horror
have poisoned the soil's breath,
have burnt the roots of gardens.

The slime of the lower depths
darkens the surface of the sea,
and the hearts of lakes
beat with longing for waves.

Think of the earth.
Kindness is being buried
and the old muezzin heralds the end.

What was the use
of so many hands?
Just to carry so many coffins?

What was the use
of so many eyes?
Just to witness
the death agony of a generation?

From the minaret-tops
one can hear cries of blood
one can hear verses of death
one can hear the grave-digger's shovel.

God's green soul
has been butchered on domes and steeples.
Think of the earth.
On tiptoe,
the night has intruded into the private gathering
of wild flowers;
and the white despair of the moon
and the hollow darkness
have spread over the desert.

Poppies

Along the battle-front, they say
the blood of the young
flows over the desert's patient soil
so that our pure, untarnished homeland
remains upright forever.

But for me
homeland was never
solely
the deserts and the plains.

Homeland is the strength of the callous hands
of the deprived.
Homeland is the pride of a child
who goes to school
with torn shoes.
Homeland is the kindness
of the hand of the carpet-weaving woman
and the sun-burnt forehead of a man
who lovingly tills the soil
and the firmness of bare feet
that leads the herd to pastures.

Homeland is the tearful eyes of a mother
who lost her four sons
in an explosion on a mine-field
and the brains
that are inspired by rifles
and not by school benches
brains whose owners
carry not books but bullets
in their school bags.

But victory shall not be yours, soldier;
it shall belong to the 'leaders'.
Soldier!
the hardness of your boots
and the ruggedness of the road
burnt your youthful skin,
and thurst your lips,
and bullets your life.

But history, this centuries-old liar,
shall remember
only the names of 'leaders'.

Tomorrow, all the short-memoried loudspeakers
will recite the wise, solemn words
of those who stole pride
from your blood-stained corpse
. . . and bread from your mother's table.
Tell me
can we ever again
expect another sunrise?

Oh, Alborz![1]
I had asked myself
on your slopes
what will grow
when the next Spring comes?
But now behold
mournful poppies
invaded by the verses of darkness.

---

[1] A mountain range in northern Iran.

Darkness

Time is at a standstill.
There is no end in sight to the road.
The stagnant journey
resembles a constant rest.

And I waste away
under the steps of restless but stationary moments.

What had we done
to deserve
such a long punishment?

What had we done
to deserve the noose of grief round our necks,
to be hanged at the gallows of frustration,
to wait forever?

This is the generation
of the bombs of hypocrisy
the generation
of the weapons of shamelessness
the generation
of the missiles of destruction
the generation
of those blown up
on the minefields of their beliefs.
Time is moving backwards.
On the steep, painful downhill of moments,
are scattered the pieces of your picture.

My dreams
are endless nightmares.
The town is adorned
with black garments of mothers.
On the streets
one can smell the rotten odour
of falsehood and deceit.

The worms
with swollen heads
are feeding on the heap of garbage
and running day-to-day affairs.

Every now and then,
the worms take the salute
while the coffins of humanity are paraded
to commemorate butcheries centuries away
to celebrate the massacre of trees.

In my dreams
there are continuous nightmares
and vibrations of a voice
that resembles the howling of an old wolf.

Clovers of love

Let the silent hills
hear the steps
that are filled with the rhythms of sensation of love
let the yellow wheat-fields
fall asleep
in the pale yellowness of sunset
with the chirping of little, kind-hearted crickets
and with the echoes of their chirping
in this vast space.

There were no hands
kinder than yours
and no glance
more magnificent than your glance
. . . the glance that dug and searched
through open horizons.

How can the little shrub
endure the night
in the silent valley?
How is the shrub to endure the night
when the clean chirping of the crickets stops
when the yellow fields of wheat
sleep calmly in the black tent of the night
and when the light scent of clovers
that awakened love
is no longer present?

The mountains are pressing the valley borders
it is as if they are advancing
step by step
with the blackness of night.
How is the little shrub to endure
an air in which clovers
no longer spread the scent of love?

Look at the road
see how it wanders,
how it seems unable to escape advancing night
although it meanders on and on.
Look at the road

see how helplessly it clings to the soil
look at that little shrub
that will be left alone
in the invasion of the night.

I wish I could bring you
the murmurings of water
in the middle of yellow wheat-fields
and the kind chirping of the cricket
in the silent valley
and all the green colours of its calm.
I wish I could give you as a gift
the kindness of all particles of soil
together with all components of nature.

You —
Memory of every goodness and kindness,
Oh, if only I could.

The abyss

Give me refuge within your little hands
when the night is the blackness of piercing eyes
   tracing me on the deserted path
   of my loneliness
when every moment is as heavy and closed as the
   moment of farewell
when I am but a shaking shadow, the turning pale
   fading of light, withstanding the weight
   of all steps with my silence.

Give me refuge within your little hands
so that the light of that lantern is endowed
   with salvation
so that the drowned withstand the abyss of whirlpools
at the confluence of two enraged floods.

What is sorrow?

Must I escape
to the cold void of books
whose heroes,
even if they suffer Christ-like crucifixion,
or even if they fade away in silent gaols,
will still leave
no load of guilt
upon my shoulders?

Must I escape
from the deep vision of scratchings and scribblings
on damp walls
from hearing the language of silence
to the printed lines on soulless paper
to the black-and-white of newspapers?

Must I escape
from dungeons
in which human beings rot away
and from a land that is burning
with the fever of ignorance?

Must I escape
and make myself content
with the cold void of books
that offer second-hand life?

Words!
You have been used so wisely and selectively
but how can I feel
the burning of the deep wounds of the soul
in your cold lifelessness?

* * *

Above so much darkness
the thick black clouds
send down their torrent of rain.
That reminds me of mothers' tears
and of the sadness of the fact
that only mothers
know the exact numbers.

I keep carrying my guilt
and my humiliating inability
upon my shoulders
I never escape
I am standing.
What pain . . . what agony.

The bazaar

Man sells fish
in order to buy clothes
for one must not be naked.

Man sells shoes
in order to buy fish
for one cannot go hungry.

Man sells meat and lettuce
in order to pay the rent
for the sky is no substitute for a good roof.

The bazaar is filled with people's hubbub
and amidst the noise
man sells lies
like rotten fish
and love
like dead flowers
and he does so boldly
for one shall live
and that is why man has been created.

In this rat-race
man even sells
his heart
his word
. . . himself.

Oh . . . life
Oh . . . destiny.

Let the heart go

I give my heart to the river
that flows
and to the clouds
that are scattered and silent.
When your eye-lids close
like the wings of a tired pigeon
and when I think that your heart
is distant and alien,
I give my heart to the river
that flows
and for whom
the clean, vast sea
with its restless waves
is waiting.

*   *   *

All blossoms
are looking at the moon
and in the dark street
no one says a word
to that lone woman
who has lost the way.
I give my heart to the river
so that it takes my heart away from the town
from a town whose inhabitants
talk to themselves
because they have no one to talk to.

You come from the horizon that is silent.
You come from the horizon that is a golden line
and, from this golden line,
I want to illuminate all roads
and give a share of light to the whole town
and bring the morning home.

Wound

That old wound opens once more
blood seeps out of the moist wound
black, warm blood
that kept me alive for years.

This old wound
had been silent for so long
without pain, without sorrow, without tears.
I was like the wound too
but
it was as if it wove a pattern of pain
behind its cold, sorrowful silence.

Today
that secret-like pain opens its mouth
that secret-like pain
that old wound
rears its head
and as I look deeply into it
I see an old cave
in whose passages
reverberate the echoes of my sighs and groans
. . . so many old melodies of past years.
This secret-like wound is a great pain on my body.
My body aches to the marrow
my black poem
flows from the wound's heart like blood.
Black, warm blood
is released
and I am relieved.

The sound of destruction

I can hear destruction of bridges
I can hear dams cracking
water will spread everywhere
water will devour our houses and our fields.

I can hear the bridges collapsing
it's not possible to go back the same way.
It's too late.
It's too late.
How can you stop
the haste of the hands on the clock?
It's too late.
Think of the little plants
along the valleys of the Alborz[1]
think of the roads
think of the fields and the nests
think of all the signs
of growth, of flight, of movement
and think of life
in my homeland.

[1] A mountain range in northern Iran.

A song for tiny hands

I now sing a new song
from the tales of life.
It is not a love story
In it, there is no trace of
soft petals
or moonlit autumn evenings
or the thirst of the desert
or morning dew-drops
or sea waves
or early evening breeze.

Here is a song
from the beatings of a tiny heart
of a small human being
with a forehead as open as the sky
with little hands holding a box
with eyes sparkling with wit
who
in the middle of the bazaar
on a summer midday as hot as in Hell
goes on hawking
with a piercing voice penetrating every ear
'cigarettes, cigarettes'.

I love my new song
I love the little hands
and the eyes sparkling with wit.

Set to depart

I saw all the windows closing
I saw the poem of my life
joining the hymn of night
I saw the sun
being imprisoned in the fortress of mountain gods
and the moon
with a broken heart
drowning the white tinge of its face
in dark, silent waters.
I saw a boat
capsizing in the claws of a strong wave.
The cries of a girl
tear apart the dark, silent heart of the night:
'I don't believe it . . . I don't believe it'.
I saw all the houses being abandoned
and I saw that no home-fire
would give me refuge any more.

This was true, this was true.
From my credulous heart
it was your love, with all its purity
that was set to depart.

Greetings to dawn

A greeting to
and a handshake with
the dawn.
A salute to the sun
I have been longing
for such a beginning
for so many years.

But for so many years
only black rain has been pouring down.
Right now
space and time
are darkened with the breaths
of foul, grim-faced clouds
and the fertile land
is captured
in the jaws of a chronic plague.

A greeting to
and a handshake with
the dawn.
A free flight
in the cradle of the wind
to the summits of snow-covered mountains
and a desire for a deep breath
in the boundless blueness of the heights . . .

So many times
I have wiped tears
from the faces of windows
but outside
the migration of the sun
is now a reality.
Do you know that we will never grow?
This, too, is a reality.

Let us tell ourselves
that a generous sprinkling of perfume
is to no avail
when even our clothes
betray the stench of falsehood.

Let us tell ourselves
that smiles
cannot hide
the rottenness of the inner self.

We need a journey
a journey along our veins
up to the pulsing of our hearts
up to an encounter with our true selves.

We need to crumble down
and to run as far as the plains
whose ends merge with the sky.

We need to crumble down
and to adjust all the minutes and seconds
on the dial of our lives
with the hands of thought.

A greeting to the dawn
and a farewell to ourselves
may yet bring a cure.

Tears

On the flaked trunk of the old pine trees
spent years are filled layer upon layer,
autumn — winter,
autumn — winter.
In the dream of branches
the little image of a nest
is aflutter.

The weight of snow presses the rooftops
the road finds its way to the town,
the town where,
breathing behind cold bars,
humanity is dreaming
of freedom.

My hands are full of tears
night is dancing outside the window
like a black phantom.

My hands are full of tears.
I will tie the wet handkerchief
to the long hair of the wind
like a flag
from the land of sorrow.

The most beautiful of all poems

Now
in a land far, far away
the green pride of tears
has advanced
as far as misty dreams of summits
and the disturbed imagination of clouds
is scattered in the blue mind of the sky.

Now
the river is bathing
in the bright spangles of waves.

Is the loneliness of the boat
on the pond of the night
and palpitations of the moon's clear heart
in the river's vein
the most beautiful of all poems?

Oh you! The loneliest of all the desert's trees!
Your hope for a rainfall
was one day in the disturbed imagination of the clouds.
Tell me, what storm blew away
the green pride of your leaves?

Oh you! The loneliest of all the desert's trees!
What use is it to you
that in a land far, far away
the greenness of trees
scratches the high forehead of mountains?
What use is it to you
that now
the red song of the wind
brings news that geraniums have been plundered?
That the wounded wings of the pigeons
bring news that nests have been burnt?

Oh you! The loneliest of all the desert's trees!
What is the most beautiful of all poems?

Search

Now you are here
but between us
mistrust is entrenched like a silent wall.
Behind this wall
my hands
burning and restless like flames
wandering like the wind
are searching your hands.

Even the wind sings your name

You are that vivid memory
you are that familiar image.
All other wishes come and go
why is it that in my heart
with the opening of every morning blossom
and with the creeping of every nocturnal shadow
you blossom once more
you appear again?

Our home, small as it is
is far from yours
but here, every night
when I open the window
my heart sees your home.
Even the wind sings your name
the curling, winding branch of the vine
knows your name
it whispers it quietly
with leaves, each a tongue.
I hear you
I hear your footsteps again
while you are passing slowly
through that long, dusty lane.
A moment later, you are in your home
and in the darkness of night
all doors close
all doors close
but the window is still open
and the wind sings your name.

Our era

The sun's burnt heart
in the heavy breathing of the sky
is the mirror of the litany of the soil.

Remember that our era
is the era of a darkness
whose dimensions
cannot be contained in words . . .
and that the dearth of love
will soon kill the young spring-time.

All blossoms of purity
have fallen to the ground
and all dew-drops of innocence
have been blown away.

Tall, proud trees!
May your thirst be quenched
by cool, sweet rain-drops.
Don't take your shade away
from this scorched body.

Our era
is the era of the dearth of consciousness
of the abundance of gallows.
It's the era of sacred offerings of people's blind hearts.
It is the era of false faith
of verses of shame
of altars bent under the weight of sins.

Our era
is the era of execution of infants yet unborn
of the chaining of breath
of man's fear of his own shadow.

Mountains of awe!
May your heights be endowed forever
with the rays of the sun.
Don't take your rain-bearing clouds
away from our feverish, thirst-stricken lands.

May the town's heart be revived
and may the silent soil
hear once again
the song of rain's happiness.

Flood of darkness

The night is cold
darkness is overflowing
from afar, one can hear the hymn of falsehood
it comes nearer and nearer
and now blows around our houses.

The flimsy paddings of laughter
can no longer hide
the mediocrity of the inside
the worm is busily eating away and destroying everything
and yet it believes it's constructing a magnificent palace.

Under the soil of what spring-time
are buried the white bodies of blossoms?
And in the depths of the swamps of what autumn
the roots of trees' lives rot away?

I wish there were a galaxy
to whose stars one could migrate
I wish the Earth were a mouth for shouting
and the sky
could carry the burden of the struggle against injustice
on its shoulders.

Come with me
come with me to a meeting with mankind
to a meeting with paralysed, miserable mankind
and place a dagger in its trembling hands
and behold how it butchers.
The voice of the oppressed is the voice of the oppressor
and the face of the oppressor
is identical to the face of the oppressed.
Behold, behold how darkness is overflowing.

Explosion

In me
something is on the verge of explosion
It is as if the walls of my vein
can no longer bear that hot fluid.

Rain into me
cloud of stormy shores
rain into me.
In this cruel wilderness
words no longer carry messages on lips
and the torn chest of the sky
has, for a long time,
been devoid of the whisperings of stars.

For how long
can eyes be given masks of laughter
when one cannot look
but through passages of torture
when the voice
is but the shouts of hawkers
whose only ware is falsehood
and the only sound heard
is that of the steps of a traveller
who, with blindfolded eyes,
passes through walled passages of no return?

Outside the walls
the rain has washed away
the footprints of passers-by
and the heart of the alley
is filled with sobbings of loneliness.

I let my heart shout
in me, something is on the verge of explosion.

In ruins

You and your world of dolls,
I and this wilderness of wandering.
A sad sunset in outlandish west.
The east submerged in the darkest of nights.
The shore is, alas, dotted with blood-stains.
The waves are revengeful and the heavens are stormy.
Our ship is caught in a whirlpool of nothingness.
The captain is blinded and deafened by ignorance.
The brains of so many youths are opened
and the snake-shouldered Astiages[1] is still looking for
                                                  new victims.
  Dawn! Break this dark night.
  I fear that we shall never reach home
  as our feet are blistered with boils and the road is too long.
  You and your world of dolls,
  I in ruins, on these ruins.

---

[1] The last king of the Medes. Legend has it that two snakes grew on his shoulders and that he had to feed them on young people's brains.

Crumbling structure

The moment the structure of the night
crumbled over the head of the sky
and the severed head of the sun
rolled on the horizon,
the song in your memory
began its resonant mourning
in the river of my veins.

* * *

I love the poor miserable land
and I am worried about the trembling hands
begging for help at a holy shrine.
In that cruel wilderness
the queue of the pilgrims of disaster
stretches as far as the blood-stained temple of sunset
and the desert wind
swallows coffins of little souls like quicksand.

We are sitting motionless.
We are sitting
making our hearts content
with the empty framework of the window.
Do you know that the blind eye-sockets of other windows
cannot carry light?
We are sitting motionless.
We are sitting
and greeting the darkness
we are sitting
and getting used to breathing an air
that is saturated with the scent of blood from our dead.

How easy it is
to accompany the coffin of another person's child.
Do you know
that the final particles of the voices of victims
cannot be contained
in 'wise' words?
in measured and well-sieved phrases?
in magnificent but meaningless sentences?

But
the final particles of the voices of victims
fill the dawn
and
begin their resonant mourning
in rivers of human veins.

Distance

We were separated
not by deserts
not by mountains, nor by oceans
but by never-ending space
and the familiar voice that filled my blood
was the echo of my own voice
coming back to me
after crossing the orbits of bright planets
and wandering through days and nights.
I thought it was his voice
but between us
were
not deserts or oceans
but unbounded space
and a heavy sky
overflowing with black sorrow
and scattered horizons of searching
and searching
until a familiar voice
would arrive down the nocturnal slope
until windows of dawn would open
and distant waters
would rise to wash the waves of light
and the open sail of the clouds
would make for dry deserts.
I am standing on top of the hill of waiting
I am sitting on the deserts of silence
on seas and oceans of turmoil
on unbounded spaces of everlasting moments of pain.
The bridges of voices are broken.
The bridges of familiar voices are broken
and in the distance
in the gap between me
and the remote reaches of unbounded space
the massive chains of despair
have stopped the movement of all bright planets.

The bridge

On the bridge
there are lines of wandering, aimless people
their elongated shadows on water
together with pieces of the moon
are riding on shoulders of waves.

On the bridge
nothing of sunshine
has remained on hands or eyes
and in the tightness of the dark cages of chests
birds of light no longer sing.
The sound of the footsteps of waves
reverberate in the crypt of time
and I find my own shadow.
It is the most aimless
among the aimless!
What will happen?
The bridge supports, with deep black cracks,
bring the thought of destruction nearer
and the burbling of waves
intermingles with the sounds of horror.

You dreamed of a plain full of poppies
full of red poppies.
In what land have they grown?
Oh, for me,
it is no longer possible
to even visualise the spring.

It is only the sound of the destruction of the bridge
the sound of crumbling
it is only the vision
of merging corpses and shadows
on waves
that get nearer and nearer.

I rain

I rain
from the black cloud of our sorrow
so that the sound of rain
sings perpetually
in the town's alleys.

And I pour down
from blossom-laden branches of love
so that the dry deserts of winter
are covered
with blood-coloured petals.

I rain
I rain
and the wind pounds my drops
onto the coldness of windows
and scatters me
into the unbounded space of love
. . . a journey to rain-drenched plains.

Abadan[1]

In the alleys of the town
the dusty wind
befriended half-open doors.
It recognised their moans
as it wandered among ruins.

In the houses
the headlines of old newspapers
were reminders
of the first day of the war
and the last night before departure.
Broken dolls
were reminders
of the lost generation.
The ripped curtains
were awaiting the sound of footsteps
that would never again be heard.
Opened ceilings
were well-acquainted with the barrage of bullets.

Write me again
the poem in which
you spoke of goodness.
All our beloved little ones
are lost in deserts far from home.
All youthful buds
have fallen on enemy's soil
and we
are the captives, prisoners of our own homeland
and we
have fallen so painfully
from our ruined skies.

Write me again
the poem in which
you spoke of goodness.

I am going to visit familiar faces
I am going to see unhealed wounds
and tombstones with no names.
I am going to see a doll

whose eye-sockets
are devoid of eyes
and full of gunpowder
I am going to see the passengers of a train
that never arrived under bombardment
I am going to see the half-open doors
in the deserted town
and the two extinguished flames of gas.
I am going to see familiar faces.

---

[1] City in south-western Iran (and site of the world's largest oil refinery) ruined in 1980 in the early stages of Iran–Iraq war.

Since the day my name was called from among the winds

They called me from among the winds
when my imagination was filled with night
and when the road was about to lose its own track
in the middle of darkness.

They called me
when no other sound was heard
than the breaking of branches
and the falling of leaves
when the cloud was but a poor, torn cover
for hiding the sufferings of the town.

Behold the reflection of the sun in window-panes
at the moment of farewell
when the widespread sunset colours the town in blood
when rooftops bear footprints of last glances.

They called from among the winds
when the sunset was widespread
and my hands were unable to feel the last of the light.
From among the winds,
it was your footsteps
that broke the silence.

Under starlight
you can live with the simplicity of a leaf
but you shall always have with you
the begging of this leaf of a hand
and, one day, one day, at the street corner
they will be burning masses of dry leaves
all that have been trampled by the townsfolk.

They called me from among the winds
as leaves are called in autumn
and my silent wandering
was devoid of even the sound of a falling leaf.

I cannot end it
and I cannot go on.
Which way is the wind blowing?
From what direction are they taking my days away?
And from what direction are they calling me?

My melted heart
is dripping down
and the sound of your footsteps
is reaching my ears
. . . like the day they called me
. . . from among the winds
. . . from among the winds.

How to love

Why do you love me?
Why do you sometimes
share moments of your life with me,
merry or boring?
Why do you think you love me?
Why do you feel obliged to ask
how I am
when you are tired of long walks
of working behind your desk
of thinking in silence?
You, who have never known
those moments when my eyes were moist and salty with
                                                      tears,
why do you sometimes think
you love me?

When I am not around,
there is conversation with someone else,
there is the cup of coffee,
there is the grey smoke of your pipe,
or there is, perhaps, the bitterness of wine.
What difference is there?
What difference is there
between drinking coffee
and tasting the bitterness of wine?
between talking to me
and sitting with someone else?

Why did you think you love me?
Love means
submission to a wave
that carries you, you know not where.
Love means
recognising one voice
in a jungle of voices.
Love means
recognising the kindness of the veins of one hand
from other hands.

Love means
constant presence of feelings,
presence of heart,
constant concentration
on one point, however vain or imaginary,
hearing a song
that you cannot hear from other branches,
feeling eternity in a single moment
and seeing the greenness of all meadows
in one small leaf.
Love means
heartache and deep sorrow.
I'd like to break the coffee cup
and the glass of wine.

Need for a journey

On the night
when the solitude of the moon
was the sorrow of the sky
and when the solitude of the sea
was the greatness of the Earth,
all little flowers learnt
how to hide the vast patience of the desert
behind their petals
and all branches with delicate thoughts
learnt
how to kindle the greenness in the buds
behind curtains of darkness.

You, thirsty dream of deserts!
the wandering howls of winds!
and the highest summits of flight!
In you,
I find the echo of my own wanderings
the dream of my own thirst
and my own need for a journey.
The silence of being at one point
puts me to shame —
not only me
but all existence.

Melody of two wings

Close the eyelid of the night
I want to worship the little flower-bed
in the twilight of the dawn
I want to fall prostrate
at the altar of the meadow
I want to begin a journey
away from myself
with the old hymns of the wind.
Place the sun
on my way
I want to learn
from the robin and the swallow,
far away from myself,
away from the heavy foulness of myself,
how to disturb the silence of the skies
with the melody of two small wings.

Illiterate

I know a man
who reads all inscriptions on ancient stones
and who knows
the grammars of all languages, dead or alive,
but who cannot read
the eyes of a woman
whom he thinks he loves.

Let there be life

The night can be filled with poems
dark, long moments can be filled with poems
— with a poem as innocent as your hands
— with a poem that, like daybreak on high summits,
has the glory of life with it.
The moment when brooks stop chanting
will not be borne
nor will the moment when I give up the struggle to move
                                                                  forward.
Going with a poem that has filled the night
and resembles the glory of dawn on high summits
is the same as flying.
Going with a poem that is written on walls all over the
                                                                    town
is the same as flying.

I will not let the mirror go dark
I will not let rain-drops find their way
to a moribund swamp
nor will I let the wandering river
be swallowed by a dead lagoon.
The end of the road is not in sight
and I am happy there will still be other horizons.

فوران حیات

با شعری می‌توان شب را پر کرد
با شعری می‌توان لحظه‌های تاریک و طولانی را پر کرد
با شعری به معصومیت دست‌های تو
با شعری که چون سپیده دم بر قله‌های بلند
جلال زندگی را با خود دارد

لحظه‌ای که صدای جویبار‌ها قطع شود
به دنیا نخواهدآمد
و لحظه‌ای که تلاش زندگی را فراموش کنم نیز

رفتن با شعری که شب را پر کرده است
و به جلال سپیده دم بر قله‌های بلندی ماند
همان پرواز است
رفتن با شعری که بر دیوارهای شهر آن را می‌نویسند
همان پرواز است

من نخواهم گذاشت که آینه تاریک شود
من نخواهم گذاشت که ریزش باران
به گردابی راکد منجا ماند
و رودخانه سرگردان را
با تلاق خاموش در خود کشد
انتهای راه نزدیک نیست
و من از اینکه افق‌های دیگری را خواهیم دید دلشادم .

Other Titles from
FOREST BOOKS

International Poetry Series

THE NAKED MACHINE Selected poems of Matthías Johannessen.
Translated from the *Icelandic* by Marshall Brement.
(Forest/Almenna bokáfélagid)
0 948259 44 2 cloth £7.95   0 948259 43 4 paper £5.95   96 pages. Illustrated

ON THE CUTTING EDGE Selected poems of Justo Jorge Padrón.
Translated from the *Spanish* by Louis Bourne.
0 948259 42 6 paper £8.95   176 pages

ROOM WITHOUT WALLS Selected poems of Bo Carpelan.
Translated from the *Swedish* by Anne Born.
0 948259 08 6 paper £7.95   144 pages.   Illustrated

CALL YOURSELF ALIVE? The love poems of Nina Cassian.
Translated from the *Romanian* by Andrea Deletant and
Brenda Walker. Introduction by Fleur Adcock.
0 948259 38 8 paper £6.95   96 pages.   Illustrated

A VANISHING EMPTINESS Selected poems of Willem M. Roggeman.
Edited by Yann Lovelock. Translated from the *Dutch*.
0 948259 51 5 £7.95   112 pages.   Illustrated

PORTRAIT OF THE ARTIST AS AN ABOMINABLE SNOWMAN
Selected poems of Gabriel Rosenstock translated from the
Irish by Michael Hartnett. New Poems translated by Jason Sommer.
0 948259 56 6 paper £7.95   112 pages   Dual text

LAND AND PEACE Selected poems of Desmond Egan.
Translated *into Irish* by Michael Hartnett, Gabriel Rosenstock,
Douglas Sealey and Tomas MacSiomoin. Dual text.
0 948259 64 7 paper £7.95   112 pages

THE EYE IN THE MIRROR Selected poems of Takis Varvitsiotis.
Translated from the *Greek* by Kimon Friar. (Forest/Paratiritis)
0 948259 59 0 paper £8.95   160 pages

THE WORLD As IF Selected poems of Uffe Harder.
Translated from the *Danish* by John F. Deane and Uffe Harder.
(Dedalus/Forest)
0 948259 76 0 paper £4.95   80 pages

SPRING TIDE Selected poems of Pia Tafdrup.
Translated from the *Danish* by Anne Born.
0 948259 55 8 paper £7.95   96 pages

SNOW AND SUMMERS Selected poems of Solveig von Schoultz.
Translated from *Finland/Swedish* by Anne Born.
Introduction by Bo Carpelan. Arts Council funded.
0 948259 52 3 paper £7.95   112 pages

FOOTPRINTS OF THE WIND Selected poems of Mateja Matevski.
Translated from the *Macedonian* by Ewald Osers.
Introduction by Robin Skelton. Arts Council funded.
0 948259 41 8 paper £6.95   96 pages. Illustrated

ARIADNE'S THREAD An anthology of contemporary Polish
women poets. Translated from the *Polish* by Susan Bassnett and
Piotr Kuhiwczak. UNESCO collection of representative works.
0 948259 45 0 paper £6.95   96 pages

POETS OF BULGARIA An anthology of contemporary Bulgarian poets.
Edited by William Meredith. Introduction by Alan Brownjohn.
0 948259 39 6 paper £6.95   112 pages

FIRES OF THE SUNFLOWER Selected poems by Ivan Davidkov.
Translated from the *Bulgarian* by Ewald Osers.
0 948259 48 5 paper £6.95   96 pages.   Illustrated

STOLEN FIRE Selected poems by Lyubomir Levchev.
Translated from the *Bulgarian* by Ewald Osers.
Introduction by John Balaban.
UNESCO collection of representative works.
0 948259 04 3 paper £6.95   112 pages.   Illustrated

AN ANTHOLOGY OF CONTEMPORARY ROMANIAN POETRY
Translated by Andrea Deletant and Brenda Walker.
0 9509487 4 8 paper £6.95   112 pages.

GATES OF THE MOMENT Selected poems of Ion Stoica.
Translated from the *Romanian* by Brenda Walker and
Andrea Deletant. Dual text with cassette.
0 9509487 0 5 paper £6.95   126 pages   Cassette £3.50 plus VAT

SILENT VOICES An anthology of contemporary Romanian women
poets. Translated by Andrea Deletant and Brenda Walker.
0 948259 03 5 paper £8.95   172 pages

EXILE ON A PEPPERCORN Selected poems of Mircea Dinescu.
Translated from the *Romanian* by Andrea Deletant and Brenda Walker.
0 948259 00 0 paper £7.95   96 pages.   Illustrated

LET'S TALK ABOUT THE WEATHER Selected poems of Marin Sorescu
Translated from the *Romanian* by Andrea Deletant and Brenda Walker.
0 9509487 8 0 paper £6.95   96 pages

THE ROAD TO FREEDOM Poems and Prose Poems by Geo Milev
Translated from the *Bulgarian* by Ewald Osers.
UNESCO collection of representative works.
0 948259 40 X paper £6.95   96 pages   Illustrated

IN CELEBRATION OF MIHAI EMINESCU Selected poems and extracts
translated from the *Romanian* by Brenda Walker and
Horia Florian Popescu. Illustrated by Sabin Balaşa.
0 948259 62 0   Limited edition £20   176 pages

THROUGH THE NEEDLE'S EYE Selected poems of Ion Milos.
Translated from the *Romanian* by Brenda Walker and Ion Milos.
0 948259 61 2 paper £6.95   96 pages.   Illustrated

JOUSTS OF APHRODITE Poems collected from the Greek Anthology Book V
Translated from the *Greek* into modern English by Michael Kelly.
0 948259 05 1 cloth £6.95   0 948259 34 5 paper £4.95   96 pages

POETRY FROM BENGAL An anthology of twentieth century Bengali poets.
Translated from the *Bengali* by Ron Banerjee.
The first book of the UNESCO Library of World Poetry.
0 948259 79 5   paper £8.95   160 pages

FISH-RINGS ON WATER Selected poems by Katherine Gallagher,
the *Australian* poet. Introduced by Peter Porter.
0 948259 75 2   paper £6.95   96 pages   Illustrated

PIED POETS An anthology of Romanian Transylvanian and Danube poets
writing in German. Translated from the *German* by Robert Elsie.
Dual text English/German. Arts Council funded
0 948259 77 9   paper £9.95   192 pages

LOVE SONNETS OF THE RENAISSANCE
Translated from the *French, Italian* and *Spanish* and *Portuguese*
by Laurence Kitchin.
0 948259 60 4   paper £6.95   96 pages   Dual text

BEFORE WE WERE STRANGERS Poems by the *American* poet Nadya Aisenberg.
Introduced by Sylvia Kantaris.
0 948259 81 7   paper £6.95   96 pages

WASTELANDS OF FIRE Poems by Ku Sang.
Translated from the *Korean* by Anthony Teague.
0 948259 82 5   paper £7.95   144 pages

STEP HUMAN INTO THIS WORLD Poems by Olaf Munzberg.
Translated from the *German* by Mitch Cohen.
0 948259 53 1   paper £6.95   96 pages

ENCHANTING BEASTS An anthology of Finnish women poets.
Translated from the *Finnish* and the *Swedish* by Kirsti Simonsuuri.
0 948259 68 X   paper £8.95   160 pages

International Drama Series

THE THIRST OF THE SALT MOUNTAIN Three plays by Marin Sorescu
(Jonah, The Verger, and the Matrix) Translated from the *Romanian*
by Andrea Deletant and Brenda Walker.
0 9509487 5 6 paper £7.95   124 pages.   Illustrated

VLAD DRACULA THE IMPALER A play by Marin Sorescu
Translated from the *Romanian* by Dennis Deletant.
0 948259 07 8 paper £6.95   112 pages.   Illustrated

International Short Story Series

RUNNING TO THE SHROUDS Six sea stories of Konstantin Stanyukovich.
Translated from the *Russian* by Neil Parsons.
0 948259 06 X paper £6.95   112 pages.

HEARTWORK Stories of Solveig von Schoultz.
Translated from *Finland/Swedish* by Marlaine Delargy and
Joan Tate. Introduction by Bo Carpelan.
0 948259 50 7 paper £7.95   144 pages

THICKHEAD AND OTHER STORIES by Haldun Taner.
Translated from the *Turkish* by Geoffrey Lewis.
UNESCO collection of representative works.
0 948259 58 2 paper £8.95   176 pages

YOUTH WITHOUT YOUTH and other Novellas by Mircea Eliade.
Edited and with an introduction by Matei Calinescu.
Translated from the *Romanian* by MacLinscott Ricketts.
0 948259 74 4 paper £12.95   328 pages

A WOMAN'S HEART Stories by Jordan Yovkov.
Translated from the *Bulgarian* by John Burnip.
0 948259 54 X paper £9.95   208 pages

THE SEER AND OTHER STORIES by Jonas Lie.
Translated from the *Norwegian* by Brian Morton and Richard Trevor.
0 948259 65 5 paper £9.95   208 pages

THE TALISMAN Stories and poems by Ganga Prasad Vimal.
Edited by Wendy Wright. G.L.A. funded.
0 948259 57 4 paper £9.95   208 pages   Dual text English/Hindi.

PREPARATIONS FOR FLIGHT Swedish stories
Translated by Robin Fulton.
0 948259 66 3   paper £8.95   176 pages